MINOR GAMES

AND RELAY ACTIVITIES

KTG know the game

Minor Games
and Relay Activities

by Robin Sykes

EP Publishing Limited

PREFACE

This book on Minor Games and Relay Activities emanated mainly from experience gained as Track Coach with Glasgow Corporation Youth Service Department. In summer they added not only variety to the programme but provided much useful work of an auxiliary nature to the various Track and Field events. In winter they were often the answer to waterlogged tracks or shortage of equipment when a Games Hall or Gymnasium was a hastily offered alternative. Obviously no claim to complete originality can be laid on behalf of this book. Many of the activities will possibly be as old as prehistoric times, may be even older! I would like to think, however, that there are some which I have developed myself and these have given me great satisfaction. More important, they have given hundreds of children immense enjoyment.

These Games and Relays can be used in schools, youth clubs, sports centres and any other organisations connected with physical education. They may be used not only as a pleasant change from the well-worn national ball games, gymnastics or swimming but also very often when time and facilities render the above impossible, due for example, to unplayable pitches, gymnasia unavailable or having to take another teacher's class at short notice. They are, of course, exceptionally worthwhile activities in their own right. The beauty of these activities is that they can be altered, adapted or improvised in dozens of permutations to suit the individual coach or teacher's own particular inclination.

Finally, my thanks are due to a great many people, sportsmen, coaches, teachers and lecturers both in this country and abroad. Their names are too numerous to mention. But most of all I am indebted to the children themselves, particularly the kids of Glasgow. To them I owe a great deal.

Robin Sykes

1. SIMPLE BALL GAMES REQUIRING LITTLE ORGANISATION OR EQUIPMENT

Zigzag Chase Ball

This game can be played inside or outside, with two teams of 4-10 people and a ball for passing per team. The object of the game is quick clean passing of the ball.

The teams arrange themselves in two facing lines, the players of one team alternating with those of the other, as in the diagram. On the signal the balls are passed up and down the line diagonally one or more times, the teams competing to complete the course first. The ball must be handled by each member of the team in turn and if dropped must be returned to the player who dropped it before continuing.

Circle Pass Out

This should be played outside or in a large sports hall, with two teams of 6-10 people and one ball such as a tennis ball or softball. A good leading-up activity for such games as softball and cricket, this is a passing and intercepting game, emphasising speed, accuracy and agility.

The central player tries to pass the ball to his or her team-mates in the outside circle approximately 10-15 yards (10-15m) from the thrower while the defending team in the inner circle 1-2 yards (1-2m) in front of the outside team try to intercept. The outside runners must move very swiftly to 'throw off' the attentions of the marking interceptors in front. This gives them space but they still must catch the ball cleanly. This, in turn, depends a lot on swift, accurate dispatches from the thrower. After a given time or a prearranged number of pass attempts the teams change over. The team with the most 'clean' catches wins.

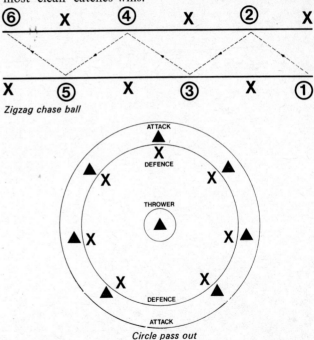

Zigzag chase ball

Circle pass out

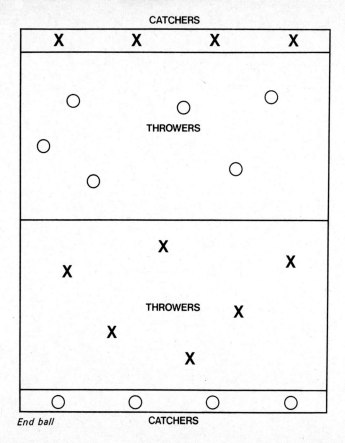

End ball

End Ball

This is best played indoors in a gym or games hall; or else the markings across an outdoor tennis court can be used. The players are two teams of 8-12 people who pass and intercept the ball, with emphasis on accuracy, speed, catching ability and agility.

The court is divided into two equal sections. A further line is drawn one yard (1m) and parallel out from the back line, as in the diagram. The players divide into two teams further subdivided into throwers and catchers (four catchers, six throwers are ideal).

The game is started by the ball being thrown in from the side line so that it bounces in the centre of the court. The throwers attempt to catch and throw it full pitch to their catchers. Each ball cleanly caught from such a throw scores a point.

The catcher then throws the ball back to his throwers who attempt to score again. The opposition throwers try to intercept passes from catchers and any pass from a catcher who has scored a point.

Throwers who find their route blocked may pass quickly to better-placed colleagues, but the ball may at no time touch the ground. There is no running with the ball. Fast running is essential 'off the ball' to create more space. Throwers must at all times stay within the limits of their court area. If the throwers drop the ball, or their throw-in is unsuccessful or goes out of play, then the ball goes to the opposing team.

Gaining ground

Nerves

Gaining Ground

Although it can be easily adapted for outdoor play, this game is best played indoors between end walls, by two teams of up to twelve people using a medicine ball, if available, for boys, or a lighter ball for girls. The aim is to hit the opposing team's wall (indoors) or to cross their line (outdoors) by powerful throws of the ball.

Without tackling or passing, or the same player throwing twice in succession for his team, the teams take turns to throw the ball, one thrower at a time, trying to force their opponents back. Opposing players must stand at least six feet (2m) from players taking their throw, and should not bunch together but spread out to cover the court (or field) in depth.

A player catching or stopping the ball throws from where he or she receives it, and should not return it into the mass of the opposition but should look for space, getting the ball as near the wall as possible. The ball may be thrown in any way at all.

As a team forces the opposition back they naturally move forward, but they should be careful to cover the court behind them as a good quick field and return from their opponents can often lose them hard-won ground.

Nerves

This simple game can be played indoors or outdoors by up to a dozen players using a small ball for throwing and catching. A tennis ball or small softball is ideal. The players try to catch the ball cleanly, one handed or two handed, without anticipatory attempts in a competition which is excellent for sharpening the reflexes.

The group form in a circle around the thrower approximately five to eight yards (5-8m) distant. There should be at least three to four yards (3-4m) between each catcher so that they are in no doubt as to whom the ball has been thrown and so that they have room to dive sideways, if necessary, for the ball.

Each player has his (or her) hands behind his back and must only bring them to the front to catch the ball. The thrower may feint to throw, without actually letting go of the ball. A catcher will be eliminated if in this case he moves his hands from behind his back. Any player dropping the ball is also eliminated. Last player remaining is the winner.

It is usually best for the teacher to act as the thrower. In this way he can make the game more exciting by varying the throws, some high, some low, some to the side and so on. He should make the throws increasingly difficult as the field narrows down to ensure a quick turnover of games—those eliminated early like to get another chance as quickly as possible, and the games must be kept 'ticking over'.

Snatch Ball

This is a game for the games hall or sports centre or, in dry weather, outdoors. The members of two teams of 4-10 players try to gather a small ball or other object (small football or rugby ball are best) and return to their line untouched by their opposite numbers. The emphasis here is on speed and agility.

As in the illustration, the teams are lined up and given numbers in reverse order. One of the numbers is called

Snatch ball

out and the player with that number from each team dashes out in an attempt to snatch the ball and get back over his or her line without being touched by the opposite number. He may go by any route he likes. For example he may run past his opponent on the way out as he grabs the ball and may even run over his opposite number's line so long as he can get back over his own line untouched. The ideal way, of course, is to get the ball first, collect it, and get back as fast as possible. The main difficulty here is that the collecting player has to change direction and must therefore be very fast.

The ball must be taken cleanly. If it is dropped the players return to their places after which any other number is called out.

If both players reach the ball in the middle at the same time the idea is not to grab for the ball, and so be touched at once, but to manoeuvre for possession. Try feinting movements in the hope of catching the opponent off balance and then snatching the ball away quickly. Remember that a player cannot be touched unless he has the ball in his hands.

Running the Gauntlet

Catering for large numbers, this game can be played in or out of doors using a tennis ball indoors or a light plastic ball outdoors which can be struck with the fist or with a bat. The object of the game is for the batter to strike the ball and score runs, the fielders trying to hit him with the ball.

The players are divided into two teams: one batting, one fielding. The fielding team may spread themselves anywhere on the court, including behind the batter. Each member of the batting team goes in turn. The ball must be bowled underhand to reach the batter between shoulder and knee, and so that it can be hit. Whether the batter hits or misses he must run.

If he reaches halfway (i.e. the outward journey) without being hit he scores 1 pt. If he gets back after the next man goes in he scores 2. A straight out and back, of course, scores the 2 pts. He need not run back when the next batter comes in. Players may wait over the 1 pt. line until they feel it is relatively safe to run. Obviously, however, it is in their own and their team's interest to get back as quickly as possible.

The ball may be thrown at any running man, either outgoing or incoming, by anyone in the fielding team. The fielding team may pass to each other if they wish but they cannot run with the ball. Three men out and the teams change over. A catch puts the batter out, but not the whole team.

Running the gauntlet

Three Court Dodge Ball

A good warm-up or concluding activity, this can be played indoors by about twenty to thirty boys in three teams, using a football or volleyball. The aim is to hit players with the ball, practising throwing and agility.

As shown in the diagram the Court is divided into three equal areas with one of the teams occupying each area. The object of the game is for players of the two end teams to throw the ball and hit the players in the middle court. The middle team attempt to avoid being hit while remaining within the boundary of their court.

The three teams occupy the centre court in turn for a specified time, and the team against which the lowest number of hits are scored is the winning team. The throwing teams may co-operate by interpassing, but no hit can be scored if they overstep their line area or run with the ball.

Passers versus Runners

This can be played in or outdoors by two teams of 5-10 people using a ball for passing. While one team passes the ball, the other runs.

One team forms a circle while the other lines up in a file. The size of the circle depends on the number of players or the amount of running which is required. A football centre circle is often ideal. The game starts with the team forming the circle passing the ball round the entire circle six times (or any chosen number). They may pass in clockwise or anti-clockwise direction.

Meanwhile the runners run round the circle, either back to where they started or over the finishing line. Each time a runner returns or crosses the finishing line the next runner goes. The runners keep running in succession until the passers have completed their circuits (so some runners may go two or three times).

Each time the passers drop the ball a run is added to the runners' score. The number of times each runner returns or crosses the finishing line is counted as a point and at the completion of the circuits the total points (including dropped passes) are added up. Teams then change over. Two to three innings are usually sufficient for this activity.

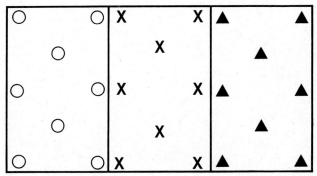

Three court dodge ball

Passers versus runners

2. MINOR GAMES REQUIRING SOME EQUIPMENT AND ORGANISATION

Deck Table Tennis

This can be played outdoors by two or four people on each court using a not-too-light plastic ball or similar. Larger numbers can be catered for by arranging a series of courts side by side. Played to the rules of table tennis this is a game with emphasis on agility.

Deck table tennis

For singles the court should be roughly thirty feet (10m) in length and twenty to twenty-four feet (6-7·2m) in width. A doubles court should be wider. A bench can be used for a net but it is possible to play the game effectively with simply a line drawn across the centre of the court. (This is very useful when playing on the beach.)

The Server must serve underhand from behind the baseline and the receiver must stand behind his baseline till the ball crosses the mid-line before he can move into court to play. Rules are exactly the same as table tennis except that the ball can be hit on the volley (i.e. without letting it bounce first) to score points.

Gym Squash

An indoor game suitable for a games hall, this is played by two or four people using tennis balls and a solid wood bat each. The object is to win points as in badminton and squash rackets.

Players serve from behind a line as in the diagram. The ball must strike the wall above the three foot (1m) line and rebound back into the area of play. Players are allowed two serves, and if both are out the service goes to the other team.

After the serve, the players hit the ball alternately until the ball bounces twice, rebounds from the playing wall out of play without bouncing, hits the roof or hits the wall below the net line.

Whoever serves must win his serve to score; scoring is as in badminton.

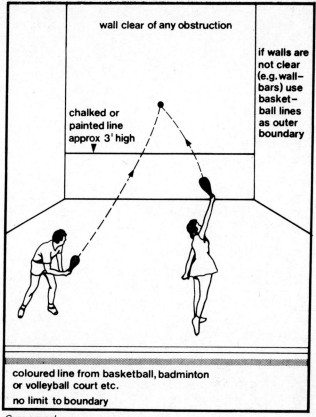

wall clear of any obstruction

if walls are not clear (e.g. wall-bars) use basket-ball lines as outer boundary

chalked or painted line approx 3' high

coloured line from basketball, badminton or volleyball court etc.

no limit to boundary

Gym squash

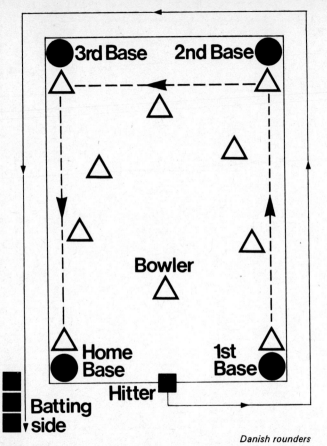

Danish Rounders

Essentially an indoor game, this is ideally suited for a badminton court marked out in the gymnasium. Outdoors, the pitch can be set by four markers at the corners. It caters for 10-30 players, using a tennis ball, the object of the game being to hit the ball and make runs.

The pitch is laid out as in the diagram. The striker must first of all hit the ball using his or her clenched fist on receipt from the bowler who must bowl underhand to him. He then tries to run round the four markers to the home base by way of the outside line in the diagram. There is no waiting at any of the bases.

In the meantime the fielding side must retrieve his hit and get the ball to the man in first base who then throws it to the man in second base. From there it goes to the third and home bases by the same method. (See inside line in the diagram.) If the ball gets back before the striker he is given out. The ball may be dropped by the fielding side at any point in the game but if it is in the hands of the home base fielder having come the proper route before the incoming runner it counts as a dismissal. If the striker gets in before the ball his team are given a run.

A catch direct from a hit renders the whole team out and the change-over then occurs.

Danish rounders

Softball

This game is an adaptation of American baseball and has much in common with the national sport of the United States, though it is usually classified as a minor game in this country. Ideally it should be played outside as a summer game in parks and playing fields, though it can be adapted for indoors. Players are two teams of 9 people and a referee. A softball and bat are needed.

The basic field positions are as shown in the diagram. Distances between bases should be approximately thirty yards (30m), and the plate, chalked or marked with sawdust, should be roughly five feet (1·5m) long and three feet (1m) wide. The bases are circles approximately three to five feet (1-1·5m) in diameter.

The pitcher should stand ten to fifteen yards (10-15m) from the striker and bowl underhand so that the ball passes across the plate between the levels of the striker's shoulders and knees. A ball which is bowled correctly but which the striker does not hit is classed as a strike. On the third strike the striker must run to the first base whether he has struck the ball or not.

If the pitcher throws outside the strike area the pitch is classed as a ball. Four of these and the striker may walk to first base.

If the striker hits the ball into the non-scoring zone neither the striker nor any team-mates occupying bases may run. If the striker hits twice in succession into this zone he is out.

If the striker hits the ball anywhere in the scoring area—infield or outfield—he must run, even if he mishits and the ball drops a few feet in front of him. To

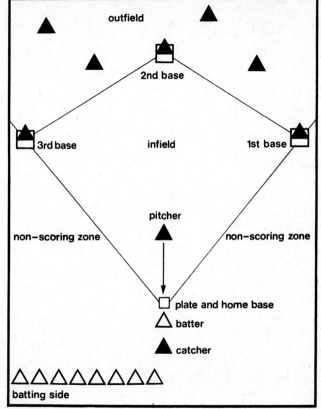

Softball

get players out the ball is thrown to the man standing on the base to which they are running. If he holds the ball cleanly with at least one foot on the base before the incoming runner arrives, then that runner is out. The idea, of course, is to get the ball to first base every time as quickly as possible, to prevent progress round to nearer the first base. A runner is 'in' at a base if one or both of his feet have touched the circle before the catcher receives the ball. Only one runner at a time may be at a base.

Each time a runner crosses the home base, whether from a home run or in stages, counts as one run. If the bases are full it is sensible to try to get the ball back to the home base to prevent the incoming runner from scoring as well as to get him out.

A catch (which may be made in the scoring or the non-scoring area) puts the whole team out, and the innings is also deemed closed when three men in the team are run out. On the subsequent innings the player who was due to bat when the innings closed goes in first.

Players may not run between bases when the pitcher is pitching, but only when the striker hits the ball. A player who runs to a base (except first) can change his mind and go back provided he has not covered more than half the distance to the base. If he has, he must run on in the hope that either he will get there before the ball or that the baseman will drop it.

Bench Basketball

Two teams of 4-8 people are suitable for this game which is best played in a gymnasium or games hall, or outside on a hard court. A variation of basketball, emphasising passing and intelligent use of space, the equipment needed are a basketball and two benches or similar supports, such as chairs or boxes.

Each team has a member standing on a bench at their opponents' end of the court. The idea is to get the ball cleanly into this player's hands, a point being scored each time this is effected. Normal basketball rules apply as regards dribbling, carrying, passing etc. As a variation the rules which apply to Head Handball (see p. 16) may also be used here.

Bench basketball

Bouncer Handball

This can be played on a hard court, inside or out, ideally by two teams of 4-6 boys. Larger numbers tend to cause congestion and leave too many players not sufficiently involved in the game. The aim is to bounce a mouldmaster or heavy plastic ball between goalposts. The pitch should be approximately thirty to thirty-five yards by twenty-five (27-31·5m × 22·5m). A good conditioning game, it encourages intelligent use of open space.

Players may keep possession by running and bouncing (basketball style) but may not run carrying the ball. A player must always pass immediately he is touched by an opponent. Players may not obstruct or overguard but may gain possession by interception or fair tackle (blocking, dispossessing whilst on the move etc.).

A jump ball is the outcome if two players get possession at the same time. If the ball goes out of play it is a throw-in to the team opposing that last playing the ball. When a goal is scored the game is re-started from the centre by throwing the ball up between two opposing players.

Bouncer handball

3. MINOR GAMES ALLIED TO FOOTBALL AND RUGBY

Head Handball

This is a game for two teams of 4-5 boys playing outside across the width of a section of a rugby or football pitch, or indoors in a games hall or sports centre. The object is to pass a football or basketball so that it can be headed into the opponents' goal, with emphasis on use of space and stamina.

Two strides are permitted with the ball before it must be passed. The ball cannot be pulled from a player's arms by opponents, who can gain possession by interceptions, saving shots, loose balls, or by their opponents putting the ball out of play.

The ball should be moved very fast end to end using rugby or basketball techniques of passing, and successful teams will be those who make the most intelligent use of support, dummy runs and positional play plus fast, intelligent running, bearing in mind the two-step rule.

A goal is scored by heading the ball into the opponents' goal either from a colleague's pass, a deflection, rebound or loose bouncing ball. A player may not pass the ball up to himself and head it. Anyone may save a shot—there is no goalkeeper as such.

At no time may the feet be used except in blocking (not kicking) possible goals at one's goal line. Infringement results in a free throw to the other team.

Playing time should be carefully regulated. As players tire and slow down, the real value of the game deteriorates and when it is veering towards walking pace it is time to finish. The game is at its best as a concluding activity, as teams will rarely keep the pace up for more than 15-20 mins.

Head handball

Soccer Tennis

This game is suitable for two teams of 4-6 players outdoors on a calm day or otherwise indoors in a games hall. A light plastic ball is needed and a court divided by a net or similar divider. The teams try to score points by returning the ball to their opponents' court, using football techniques.

The ball is served by each member of the team in turn from anywhere behind the base line into the opponents' court, either by heading, chipping or bouncing the ball first then kicking it over. It may fall anywhere within the court and may be returned on the volley or after one bounce but not more. The ball may be returned by use of head, foot or knee, but hands are not permitted. Scoring is by the same means as in badminton, i.e. only when serving can a team score a point.

Crab Football

Two teams of 4-6 boys can play this indoors in a gymnasium or outside in dry conditions. The aim is to score goals with a football, using football techniques, but keeping hands on the ground.

Players must adopt the 'crab' position and may only play the ball in this fashion. They can move as fast as they like by pushing with the hands and sliding the seat along the floor or by raising the seat and travelling on hands and feet. At least one hand, however, must always be in contact with the ground.

The goalkeepers may adopt the kneeling position and are the only players permitted to do this. Infringements result in free kicks. Throw-ins, goal kicks or throw-outs may be taken if there are boundaries being used. In the normal school gymnasium it is usual to make play continuous by allowing the ball to remain in play when it rebounds from the walls.

Soccer tennis

Crab football

Touch rugby

Touch Rugby

This can be played indoors or, ideally, outside across a half rugby or football pitch marked with corner flags. It is suitable for two teams of 4-8 boys or girls using a football, plastic ball or rugby ball etc. A conditioning game with emphasis on stamina, the object is to carry the ball untouched over the opponents' goal line. There is no need, unless so desired, to touch the ball down.

The ball must be kept off the ground at all times and should be passed out in a line similar to the actual game of rugby itself. It is best to insist on passing the ball backwards. This avoids members standing up near their opponents' line and the players getting mixed up amongst each other. If a player in possession is touched or his team drop the ball, then the ball goes to the other team.

To re-start after an infringement the team in possession should line up across the pitch behind the player with the ball who re-starts by passing the ball out. Meanwhile the opposing team should retire at least ten yards (10 m) to allow the team in possession to get going. There is nothing to stop a player passing immediately to one of his team-mates before any line-up if he feels there is an advantage to be gained.

Players should run hard with and without the ball. If the line ahead is clear go for it because, even if caught, the team is that much nearer opponents' line. Backing up is essential because if a player is about to be touched he can do nothing but pass the ball and support for this is a must. There is no kicking ahead. Avoid bunching, as this makes defence easier for the opposing team. Spread out, pass the ball about, try to find space, and above all, both in defence and attack—run!

A variation is Two or Three Touch Rugby, where a team may keep possession for two or three touches before submitting the ball to the opposition.

4. SIMPLE RELAYS WITHOUT EQUIPMENT

Boat Race Relay

A squatting relay suitable for teams of 6-8 people, this is useful for the development of the quadriceps muscles.

The teams line up, each member squatting and holding the team-mate in front by the waist. Each team has a leader who stands facing his team and grasps the first member by the hands or wrists. On the signal to commence, the leader starts to walk backwards, and the idea is for his team to bounce forward in unison with him until the last man has crossed the pre-determined finishing line. A team is disqualified if any member does not squat down properly or there is any breaking of the linking chain.

Boat race relay

Team carrying relay

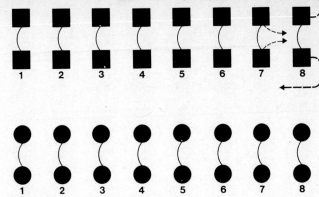

Tunnel relay

Team Carrying Relay

A good warm-up activity and leg-strengthening exercise, this piggy-back racing can cater for large numbers.

Teams line up in file behind a starting line facing the direction of the finishing line set at a pre-selected distance in front of them. On the starting signal the second man jumps on the back of the first who runs carrying him to the line in front. Having crossed the line the second man drops off and runs back to carry the third man in the same fashion whilst the first man forms up over the finishing line. The winners are the first team to form themselves up facing back down towards the starting line. The whole process is quite simple. The man who has carried stays over the finishing line, the man who has been carried goes back for the next man.

The idea is for the biggest and heaviest man to go first in the carrying. See how many teams arrange themselves intelligently according to size and weight thereby ensuring maximum speed. See also how many end up by having their smallest and lightest going back for the last man who also happens to be the biggest and heaviest!

Tunnel Relay

This simple relay caters for large numbers in teams of couples.

Teams line up in couples holding inside hands to form arches. The first couple turn outward, race down the outside of their own file, round the last couple and back to their places under the arches. The second couple starts immediately the first couple has returned to place, passing under the arch made by the first couple.

Joining-on Relay

Again catering for large numbers, this relay needs teams of 4-6 members.

Teams are arranged in line, and there should be marks for the first and last players to toe. On the signal the last player runs out to his left, round the first player, back across his starting line then joins on to the player in front (i.e. the second to last player in the original line up), holding him by the waist. They then both follow the same route once more this time with the 'picked up' player leading (see diagram). Finally the first player is picked up, leads over his own line, runs round the back line and returns with the whole team intact to stop on his own line once more. There must be no breaking of contact once players have joined on. First team back in its original starting position is the winner.

The game can be repeated by facing the players round the other way on completion so that each gets a turn of leading by changing direction and places. Variety can be added by altering points of hold (shoulders, waist) or adopting squat or hopping positions.

Wheel Relay

Four teams of any number are needed for this relay.

Teams are formed up as in the diagram. Size of circle and number of players can be adjusted according to requirements. The race starts with the first member of each team running in a clockwise direction round the 'wheel' established by the formation of the four teams. Each runner covers three-quarters of the clock, coming

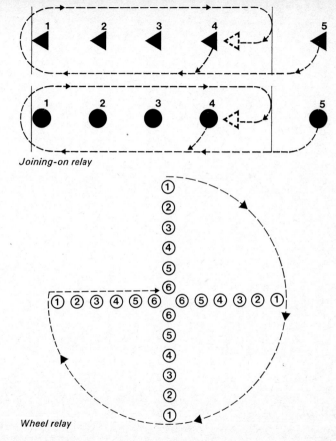

Joining-on relay

Wheel relay

in at the tail end of his own team. In the meantime each member of his team will have moved up one place. This process continues until the entire team is back in its starting position. The first team back in its starting formation is the winner.

This relay requires careful balancing of ability amongst teams otherwise front runners may catch up on the tail of the team nearest them.

A variation of the game is to introduce the carrying and passing of a ball.

All-in Zigzag Relay

Teams of any number can play this game which emphasises agility and running ability.

Teams line up in file with the No. 1 men in each team remaining still throughout. The idea is to transfer your runners as shown in the diagram, starting with the last man in each team first.

For example, No. 6 runs round No. 5 on his way to take his or her place in front of No. 1. As he passes No. 5 he is joined by No. 5, and on passing 4 is joined by him, and so on, so that the whole team is running at the same time. The team lining up in reverse order (as in diagram) first is the winner.

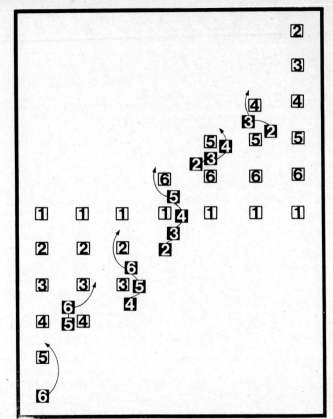

All-in zigzag relay

5. SIMPLE RELAYS REQUIRING SOME EQUIPMENT

Bench Relay

Any number of people, divided into teams, can play this simple relay. Each team will need a bench or similar object for carrying, as shown in the diagram.

Each team begins by sitting astride a bench. On the starting signal they get up and run with the bench, legs still astride it, until they reach the finishing line.

They then turn round to face the other way and do exactly the same thing on the way back. First team back to its original starting place (and facing the direction in which they started) is the winner.

A variation is the 'conveyor belt' bench relay. The teams carry the bench above their heads, pushing it in front as they walk forwards. When the last man loses touch of the bench he runs round to the front of his team. This process is repeated each time the bench passes over the head of the last man. The peeling off men may **run** but the team must **walk.** First team over finishing line is the winner.

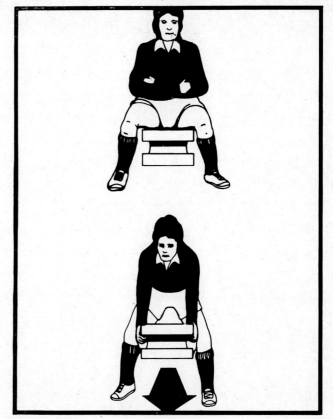

Bench relay

Tunnel ball relay

Tunnel Ball Relay

This can be played by teams of any number using a ball (preferably a medicine ball) per team.

Teams line up in file with the front person in each team holding the ball. On the starting signal the first player passes the ball back under his or her legs, and the ball is then propelled through the legs of all the team who are standing, legs astride, behind him.

The last player gathers the ball and returns to the front position where the entire process is repeated. The winning team is that which has its original starting player back in his place first.

Variations: the winners can be the team leading after a certain time or it may be that the team moves forward after the ball has passed under the legs so that the winning team is that which has all its members over the starting line first. Alternatively the ball may be passed first time between the legs, next time over the top of the head backwards, then through the legs again, and so on.

Time Ball

This is a game for any number of players divided into teams, using a ball per team.

Teams line up in file with two yards (2m) space between each player and approximately five to six yards (5-6m) behind a starting line. Each team has a leader who stands on the other side of the starting line facing his team. On the starting signal the leader throws a ball (rugby, basketball, football) to the first member of the team who, on catching the ball, runs round the back of his team and on returning to his place throws the ball back to the leader and sits down. The leader throws the ball to the second member of the team who does the same thing. When it comes to the last man he simply receives the ball from the leader, throws it straight back to him and sits down.

First team sitting down with the ball in the leader's hands is the winner.

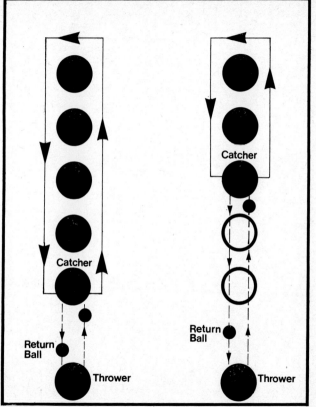

Time ball

Ball Carrying Relay

This is a game for teams of any number, each of which needs a ball for throwing and catching.

The teams line up in file behind the starting line, first man holding the ball. On the starting signal he runs to a predetermined line, turns round and throws the ball back to the next man before moving back a place to allow the next runner to do the same. This process is repeated right through the team except for the last man who need only catch the ball and bring it over the line to join his team.

Winners are the first team lined up (in reverse order, of course) with the ball in the last man's hand.

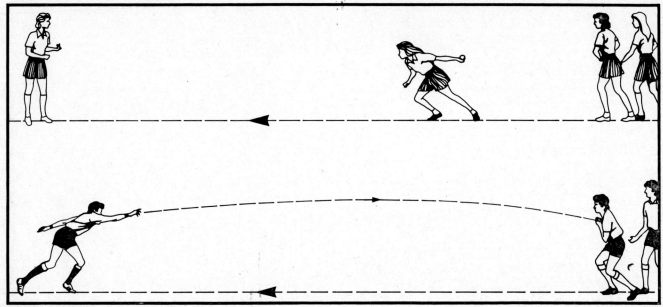

Ball carrying relay

Corner Spry

Teams of 4-8 players are needed and a ball for throwing and catching.

The players in each team line up facing their No. 1 as shown in the diagram. On the starting signal the No. 1 throws the ball to the No. 2, who is always on his left. No. 2 throws it back to him whereupon he then throws it to No. 3 and so on right down to the last man.

When the ball reaches the last man, however, he does not return it but comes out to take the place of the leader who moves to take the place of the first player as the whole lines moves down one place. The game is continued under the new leader. This is repeated until each player in the team has had a turn of being leader and the players have worked their way back to their original positions, the original No. 1 being back out in front of his team again. Team lined up first wins.

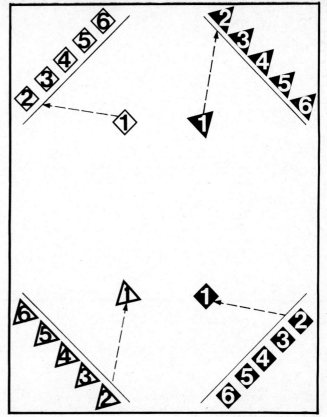

Corner spry

Down and back relay

Down and Back Relay

Teams of any number can play this game, each team needing a football, rugby ball or similar.

The teams line up in file, and on the starting signal the first man runs to a predetermined line carrying the ball. He places it down just over the line and returns as quickly as possible to the next man who runs when he is touched by the incoming runner. The second runner goes down, picks the ball up and brings it back, transferring it to the third man at the starting line. The third man then does the same as the first and so on. So it is an alternate process of taking down and bringing back. Ensure that the ball is placed down firmly, otherwise it may roll away, making things difficult for the next runner.

The winning team is the first one lined up in its original position, leader holding the ball. The contest may also be decided on a time basis, the winners being the team leading after three minutes or so.

Pick Up and Pass Relay

An excellent outdoor leading-up activity, this game is especially useful in encouraging young beginners to pass the rugby ball backwards. It requires teams of any number, with a football or rugby ball per team.

Teams line up behind starting line A as shown in diagram. Each team has a passer midway between lines A and B. The relay starts with the passer, No. 1, dropping the ball on the ground or passing it by foot slightly backwards towards his own team. No. 2 then runs out to collect, either picking up (rugby ball) or collecting (football), goes past No. 1 then gives the ball back to him before continuing on to cross line B and back to the end of his team. First team back to original places wins.

The relay can be made continuous by giving every player a chance at passer. This involves the passer leaving the ball in the middle after the last man has played. The last man then returns only to the middle and the relay continues until the whole team has been involved in both passing and running.

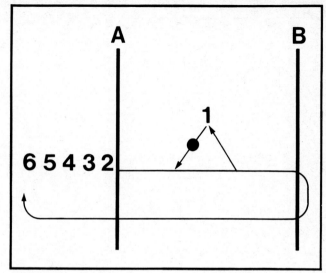

Pick up and pass relay

Pursuit race

6. ADJUNCTS TO TRACK AND FIELD TRAINING

Pursuit Race

This is an excellent concluding activity for outdoor track sessions catering for any number of runners round a track or similar course. The aim is simply to run the course without being overtaken.

The runners line up in single file. The coach or teacher taps the first runner on the shoulder as the signal to run. He then starts the other runners at chosen intervals until they are all running at the same time. Whether the run is round the track or a given circuit (football pitches, tennis courts etc.) the idea is to pass the runners in front without being overtaken from the rear—Pass but don't be Passed! Runners overtaken drop out and return to the starting point. Those who succeed in crossing the finishing line are deemed successful.

With practice the coach becomes adept at 'handicapping' the runners and putting the fastest boy in last. There are, of course, always the dodgers who contrive to be overtaken in the early stages. The prospect of a second or third run for the 'losers' usually encourages greater effort.

Hopping to the Pit

This is an outdoor game requiring a broad or triple jump pit and runway, though it can easily be adapted to other situations. The players are teams of any number who are to hop a length of ground—an excellent leg strengthener and specific practice for jumpers.

Equal teams are lined up at opposite ends of the runway, as shown in the diagram, making sure that distances are similar. On the starting signal the first member of each team hops down to the pit trying to reach the sand with the minimum number of hops. When he has done so the second member goes, and so on till the entire team has taken part. The team with the least number of total hops is the winner.

Various alternative methods of jumping etc., may be used, e.g. consecutive standing broad jumps, steps instead of hops landing on alternate feet each time, or a combination of hops and steps, and so on.

Care should be taken to rake the pit regularly as quickly as possible between jumps as all the jumpers are likely to be landing in much the same area just at the start of the sand. It is also best to ensure that the pit is a long one, so that there is no risk of collision in the middle. An alternative arrangement is to have teams coming in along one side of the pit rather than down the runways. Extra teams can be catered for in this way.

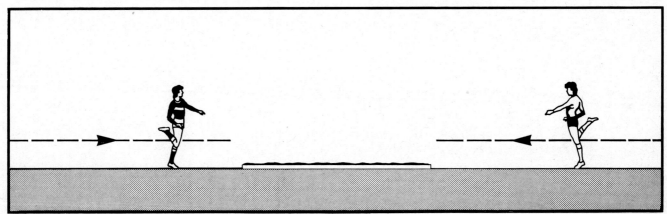

Hopping to the pit

Obstacle Course Relay

An adjunct to childrens' Track and Field training, the aim of this game is for individuals to get round a circuit of obstacles as quickly as possible. It can be played in or out, caters for any numbers, but requires a fair amount of equipment to form the obstacles.

A typical course is laid out in the diagram, the letters referring to the following obstacles:

A The starting point. 2-3 High Jump/Pole Vault landing beds placed together lengthwise.
B Steeplechase barrier
C 2 hurdles
D 4 chairs or other obstacles
E 2 hurdles
F Steeplechase barrier
G 2 hurdles
H High jump bar approx. 2ft. 6in. (0·75m) in height
I 3 benches
J 1 or 2 high-jump landing beds.

The single line dotted is a full lap of the Track, the line a shorter one for younger members. Whether children go over or under barriers is up to the discretion of the teacher. Teams line up at the side of the starting point (A) and the outgoing runner leaves when his hand is touched by the incoming runner who, in this circuit, can gain distance by a final dive. (Most children enjoy this bit!)

The course can be altered or adapted according to the coach, and a variety of alternatives can be employed. For example, horizontal jumping pits could be utilised if in the vicinity (for hopping through the sand, for instance), or the hurdles could be laid out three or four in succession as in a race. Part of the course could be confined to hopping or continuous standing broad or triple jumps. The above course is merely a guide, and is wide open to any permutations which the coach may wish to improvise.

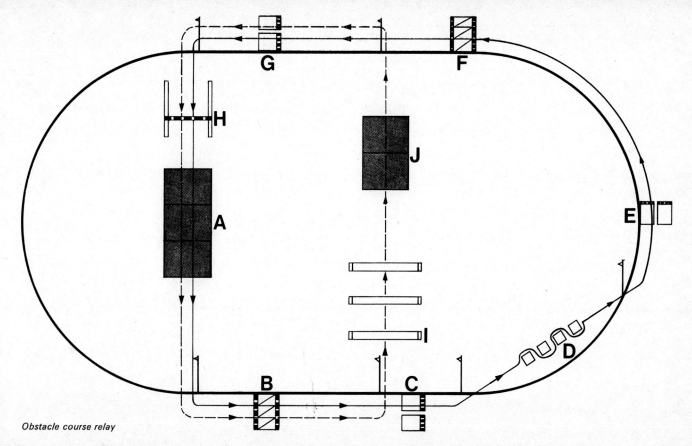

Obstacle course relay

1st Jumper

2nd Jumper

3rd Jumper

Climbing the ladder

Climbing the Ladder

The object of this game is to cover ground in standing jumps, hops and so on, as part of athletics training. It can be played by any number of people, inside or outside, and requires no equipment.

Teams line up in file behind the starting line. On the starting command the first member does a standing broad jump as far forward as he can. The second member of the team comes out and places his toes on the spot where the first man's heels landed and does exactly the same. The procedure is then repeated for the third man, and so on till the entire team have jumped. The team with the longest ladder are the winners.

Outdoors the teams may jump three or four times if required, allowing each member greater participation; but indoors it is likely that one jump each would be all that could be undertaken.

The competition can be adapted to utilise, for example, a standing triple jump for each member, or three standing broad jumps, three hops, or any other jumping combination which the coach may wish to utilise.

Assorted Activities

This is an ideal competition for a large class (30-50 boys and girls) in a normal school gymnasium, using the basic gym equipment. The class is divided into six groups of 6-8 pupils, each group attempting to get the highest possible score within the space of two minutes at their own particular activity. They then move on in clockwise direction to the next activity, and so on until the circuit has been completed. Scores are recorded (preferably on a blackboard so that the class can see how the competition is going) and final placings arranged accordingly.

Activities listed here and shown on the diagram are only meant to act as a rough guide. Many variations could be employed.

1. Form a circle and pass a medicine ball around as many times as possible.
2. Travel along the beams using overgrasp, jump off run along the bench as shown and return to end of queue at beam starting point. Each return counts as one point.
3. Group lies on its back, tucks feet under wall-bars and does as many sit-ups as possible within the two-minute period. Team's total is the recorded score.
4. Bottom section of the box lined up against the wall. Team stands behind a fixed line and kicks the ball in turn trying to get it to rebound from within the section. Each shot on target scores a point.
5. Over and under the two bucks and back along bench. Each return to start gets a point.
6. Standing broad jump. As shown, one point for an average jump, two for a good one and three for an outstanding distance. Distances determined by the teacher's discretion according to the class's ability. Group takes as many jumps as they possibly can within the two-minute spell.

The scoring table is shown below. Each box is divided into two sections, the left hand for the score the right one for points allotted. The last two boxes are for total points and final placing of each group according to order of merit.

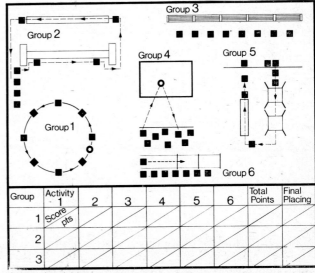

Assorted activities

7. CIRCUITS SUITABLE FOR ATHLETICS, FOOTBALL AND RUGBY

Athletic Circuit

Suitable for a gymnasium or games hall, the beauty of this athletics training competition is that it can cater for large numbers of boys and girls (in teams of 3-6) and requires very little equipment. Tasks may, of course, be altered or improvised to suit needs, but as a rough guide the circuit shown on the diagram may be used.

1. A number of benches (or hurdles) set out as shown. Each member of the team runs down and back one after the other, and each completed run counts as one point.
2. This is a standing triple jump. Each member competes in rotation, scoring one point if he reaches the first line, two for the second and three for the farthest away. The team's total is added up at the end of the activity.
3. The high jump. Points are awarded for a set range of heights (e.g. 4ft. 9in. (1·42m) = 2pts., 5ft. 0in. (1·50m) = 3pts., 5ft. 3in. (1·58m) = 4pts., and so on. The team can either leave the bar at the lowest height and try to get as many jumps as possible or raise the bar for greater number of points. Some of the team may fail at this higher level, however, and points are only awarded for clearances. This is where intelligent application comes in.
4. A rope and medicine ball. Each member runs out in rotation from the side wall carrying the medicine ball. He leaves it down at the rope, climbs up the rope, comes down, picks up the medicine ball again and returns to the wall, giving the ball to the next member of the team. One point is scored each time the medicine ball is returned to the next member of the team.
5. A heavy medicine ball or covered shot (if in games hall). The scoring method is similar to (2), i.e. one point if the member reaches the first line, four if he reaches the wall, etc., members going in rotation.

The time allowed on each activity can be regulated either by watch (e.g. 2 mins. each activity in rotation) or be governed by the hurdles (e.g. after each man has run twice over the hurdles the activities stop and change round). This is a good incentive to 'go for the hurdles', as the quicker they are completed the less time the others have to complete their various tasks. In fact the whole essence of the circuit is speed (as many jumps, runs and throws as possible in the allotted time).

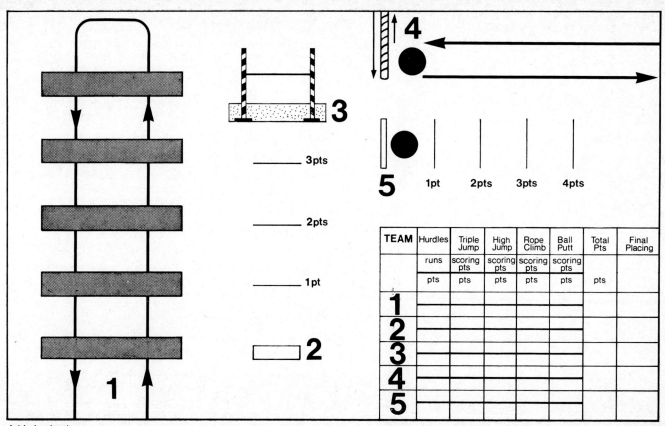

3pts

2pts

1pt

2

1

4

5   1pt   2pts   3pts   4pts

TEAM	Hurdles	Triple Jump	High Jump	Rope Climb	Ball Putt	Total Pts	Final Placing
	runs	scoring pts	scoring pts	scoring pts	scoring pts		
	pts	pts	pts	pts	pts	pts	
1							
2							
3							
4							
5							

Athletic circuit

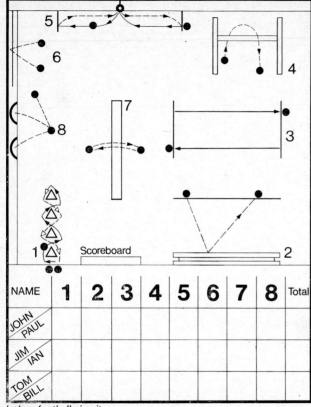

Indoor football circuit

NAME	1	2	3	4	5	6	7	8	Total
JOHN / PAUL									
JIM / IAN									
TOM / BILL									

Indoor Football Circuit

A specialist indoor activity for a small number of boys which requires a fairly extensive range of equipment, this is excellent training for football skills.

The boys are divided into pairs, each pair starting at one of the activities so that the whole class are performing at the same time. Two minutes are allowed for each activity, at the end of which each pair moves round in an anti-clockwise direction.

The activities shown on the diagram are as follows:

1. Four skittles, balls, chairs or other obstacles. The first man dribbles the ball in and out of the obstacles as shown and returns to the second man who does the same. The ball must be brought back over the starting line each time before the next person goes. One point is scored for each completed run.

2. This is simply a bench turned on its side. From behind a fixed starting line the pair pass the ball to each other on rebound from the face of the bench. Players must at all times stay behind the line. Passes which do not come back over the starting line do not count. One point is scored for each correctly effected pass.

3. A simple exercise in the 'weighting of passes'. Two chalk lines are drawn (or one may use any fixed lines such as Badminton court etc.) and the pair just simply pass the ball backwards and forwards to each other over the lines. Passes which fall short do not count. Each time a ball goes over a line counts as one.

4. A beam fixed at a height of approx. 6-7 feet (1·8-2·1m). Players head the ball to each other over the

beam. There is no starting line or any other limitation. Each time a player heads the ball the pair score one point. If the ball is dropped or out of control they simply start again. It is the total number of *consecutive* passes without any break which counts.

5. Two boundary lines equidistant from a basketball ring (or any similar improvised suspension utilising towel, tracksuit etc.). On the starting signal the first player runs out, jumps up to head the basket, carries on to the line then turns round and returns, heading the basket on the way back. When he comes back to the starting line his partner does the same. Each lap, i.e. out and back, counts as one point.

6. This is similar to exercise 2 except that it is against a wall and the ball must go above a certain height. Three feet (1m) is suggested in this instance.

7. Chipping practice over a bench or similar obstacle. To make it more difficult the recipient must trap the ball *first time* each time he receives it. Each chip and trap counts as one, though these need not be successively.

8. Practice for heading accuracy. Two circles approximately three feet (1m) in diameter are chalked on the wall, one high and one lower. One partner feeds the other who must stand at least six feet (2m) from the wall, and if the ball is headed into the top circle it scores one point, if into the bottom two points. Players change at the halfway point, e.g. one minute.

At the end of each two-minute period the scores are entered on a blackboard, as shown in the diagram. The pair with the highest score at the finish are the winners.

Rugby Circuit

This is a specialist indoor activity catering for 10-15 boys as part of their rugby training. Equipment needed are landing mats, rugby balls, chair and buck or similar obstacle.

The exercises can be modified according to circumstances, but the basic activities, as shown in the diagram, are as follows. The boys are in pairs.

1. One player stands on a high-jump landing mat or similar soft surface holding a rugby ball. The other player runs out from the wall, tackles the player in possession, takes the ball from him and runs to the opposite wall. Having touched the wall he then makes a dive pass to his partner from the mat, his partner having meanwhile taken up position at the other wall, i.e. the starting point. The ball is immediately returned to the player who made the dive pass and the whole circuit begins again with the players having this time changed positions. Each completed circuit (i.e. after the dive pass) counts as one.

2. One player stands on a bench, chair or similar elevated object. He holds the ball above his head at a height which will make his partner jump as high as he can. The partner jumps up, gets possession of the ball, and gives it back to his partner immediately. Each completed return of the ball counts as one. Players can change any time the jumper begins to slow down.

3. Just simply passing the ball back and forward over a given distance. Players must stand behind a pre-

Rugby circuit

arranged starting line. If the ball is dropped they must start again. Total number of passes between players to count.

4. One dashes out to a mat, smothers the ball, gets up and returns it to his partner. His partner simply returns the ball to him, whereupon he places it on the mat again. He then runs to the wall and his partner does exactly the same practice as just completed. Each time a player returns to the wall counts as one.

5. Kicking the ball to each other over a buck, horse etc. Players must stand behind a set retaining line. If the ball is dropped start again. Total number of consecutive passes strung together counts as final score.

The scoring table is self-explanatory. Names go in the left-hand column. For each exercise the score goes in the top diagonal section and the subsequent points according to ranking in the bottom. Final points and position go in the extreme right-hand column.

Name	Ex.1	Ex.2	Ex.3	Ex.4	Ex.5	Position
JOHN ROB	5 / 3pts					
PAUL JIM	8 / 4pts					
BILL JOE	4 / 2pts					
PETE SAM	5 / 3pts					

JOSEPH WARD & CO. (PRINTERS) LTD. DEWSBURY